Oprah Winfrey Born Jan. 29, 1954 in Kosciusko, Mississippi, Oprah W...id
...ntertainment and also in the eyes of the public. She has a personal for...s.
...prah owns her own production company, which creates feature films, ...n
...ccomplished actress, she won an Academy Award nomination.

...ooker T. Washington (1856-1915) Booker T. Washington was an educator and was the founder of the Tuskegee ...nstitute in 1881. As one of the greatest influences on American and African-American History, he was a great leader in ...reedom, self-reliance and believed in advancement through education.

...olin Powell was born in New York City on April 5, 1937. General Powell served as chairman of the Joint Chiefs of Staff, ...epartment of Defense, from 1989-1993 under Presidents Bush and Clinton. The son of Jamaican immigrants, Powell was ...ised in the South Bronx. He was educated in the New York City public schools and at City College of New York. He became ...cretary of state for the United States in 2002.

...ichael Jordan was born Feb. 17, 1963 in Brooklyn, New York. He was a five-time NBA Most Valuable Player and became ...e second person to score more than 3,000 points in a single season. Michael Jordan became a basketball team owner and ...ought basketball popularity to an all-time high.

W.E.B. Du Bois (1868-1963) A historian, sociologist, writer and civil rights activist, Du Bois was the foremost African-American intellectual of the 20th century. He worked with others to establish the National Association for the Advancement of Colored People.

Madam C.J. Walker (1867-1919) Born Sarah Breedlove, she was an entrepreneur and founder of a successful hair care products company and beauty school. Madame Walker developed a nationwide network of 5,000 sales agents — mostly African-American women — and became America's first African-American female millionaire.

John H. Johnson (1918-2005) A writer and publisher, Johnson was the head of one of the most prosperous and powerful publishing companies in the U.S. He started with the Negro Digest in 1942 and Ebony in 1945. Johnson wrote his autobiography in 1993 and won awards from numerous colleges and universities.

Find your way to The North Pole!

START

Matthew Alexander Henson
(1866-1955) A seaman, explorer, surveyor and author, Henson was the first African-American man to reach the North Pole.

Solution from pg 15:

5

Harriet Tubman (1820-1913) An abolitionist and humanitarian, Tubman became famous as a "conductor" on the Underground Railroad during the turbulent 1850s. Her life was a testimony to the fierce resistance of African-American people to slavery.

Frederick Douglass (1818-1895) One of the foremost leaders of the abolitionist movement, Douglass fought to end slavery within the United States in the decades prior to the Civil War. He provided a powerful voice for human rights during this period in American history and is still revered today for his contributions against racial injustice.

Martin Luther King, Jr. (1929-1968) One of the world's best-known advocates of nonviolent s̶o̶
change, King was a civil rights leader. He led the march on August 28, 1963 that attracted
more than 250,000 protestors to Washington, D.C. There, he delivered his famous
"I Have a Dream" oration. During the year following the march, King's renown
as a nonviolent leader grew, and in 1964, he received the Nobel Peace
Prize. In 1986, King's birthday,
January 15th, became a federal
holiday celebrated the third Monday
in January.

arbara Jordan (1936-1996) An educator, civil rights/human rights activist, state legislator and ttorney, Jordan was bestowed the nation's highest civilian honor in 1994. She was awarded the Presidential Medal of Freedom for her distinguished public service career.

Barack Obama (born 1961) is an American politician serving as the 44th President of the United States. He is the first African American to hold the office. First elected to the presidency in 2008, he won a second term in 2012. Born in Honolulu, Hawaii, Obama is a graduate of Columbia University and Harvard Law School.

Answers to page 15

1. Duke Ellington
2. Sidney Poitier
3. Thurgood Marshall
4. Harriet Tubman
5. Martin Luther King, Jr.
6. Venus & Serena Williams
7. Mary McLeod Bethune

Jesse Owens (1913-1980) A track and field athlete and long-standing Olympic record-holder, Owens is most famous for his performance during the 1936 Olympic games in Berlin, Germany.

Marian Anderson (1902-1993) A singer, Anderson was regarded during her career as the world's greatest contralto. She could sing soprano, alto, tenor and bass. Anderson's voice took h[er] around the world. She was named to the United States delegation to the United Nations in 195[8].

rena **Williams** (Born September 26, 1981) Williams is regarded by some commentators, sports ters, and current and former players as the greatest female tennis player of all time. She also n doubles grand slam titles with her sister, Venus.

nus **Williams** (Born June 17, 1980) She is also regarded as the best grass court player of her neration and is widely considered as one of the all-time greats of women's tennis. Williams is the st African-American woman to win consecutive Wimbledon Championships. Both sisters have won d medals in the Olympics.

Jackie Robinson (1919-1972) Robinson was the first African-American baseball player to win the "Most Valuable Player" award in 1949. As a professional baseball player with the Dodgers (1947-1956), he was the first African-American to play major league baseball in the 20th century.

Word Search

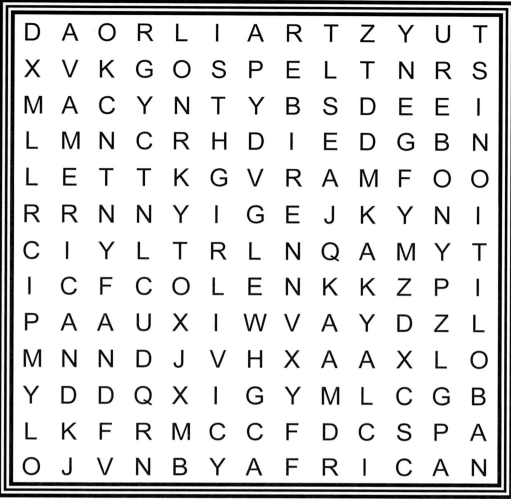

D	A	O	R	L	I	A	R	T	Z	Y	U	T
X	V	K	G	O	S	P	E	L	T	N	R	S
M	A	C	Y	N	T	Y	B	S	D	E	E	I
L	M	N	C	R	H	D	I	E	D	G	B	N
L	E	T	T	K	G	V	R	A	M	F	O	O
R	R	N	N	Y	I	G	E	J	K	Y	N	I
C	I	Y	L	T	R	L	N	Q	A	M	Y	T
I	C	F	C	O	L	E	N	K	K	Z	P	I
P	A	A	U	X	I	W	V	A	Y	D	Z	L
M	N	N	D	J	V	H	X	A	A	X	L	O
Y	D	D	Q	X	I	G	Y	M	L	C	G	B
L	K	F	R	M	C	C	F	D	C	S	P	A
O	J	V	N	B	Y	A	F	R	I	C	A	N

African
Abolitionist
Activist
American
Civil Rights
Ebony
Gospel
Jazz
Leader
Olympic
NAACP
Railroad
Slavery
Underground

(Solution on page 5)

Match the accomplishments to the correct person.

1. _____ was a famous composer, bandleader and pianist.

2. _____ was the first African-American to win an Oscar award.

3. _____ was the first African-American to be appointed as an associate justice of the United States Supreme Court in 1967.

4. _____ an abolitionist, spy and scout. She became famous as a "conductor" on the Underground Railroad during the turbulent 1850's.

5. _____ a civil rights leader and one of the world's best-known advocates of nonviolent social change. He was also famous for the "I Have a Dream" oration.

6. _____ sisters who are two of the best tennis professionals in the world.

7. _____ was an educator and co-founder of Bethune-Cookman College and was the founder of the National Council of Negro Women.

(Answers on page 11)

Duke Ellington (1899-1974) As a compose[r], bandleader and pianist, Ellington emerge[d] as distinctive, employing the rhythm[s] harmonies and tones of jaz[z] to create pieces that vivid[ly] captured aspects of th[e] African-Americ[an] experienc[e]

Sidney Poitier (Born Feburary 20, 1927)
Poitier is the first African-American to win an Oscar.
This occurred in 1963 when he received
the best actor award for "Lillies of the Field".
He holds dual citizenship in the Bahamas and U.S. and
was appointed the Bahamas' Ambassador to Japan.
Poitier also has six siblings and six children.

Jackie Joyner-Kersee (Born 196[...]
Ranked among the all-time greatest
athletes in the women's heptathlon as [...]
as in the women's long jump. She wo[...]
three gold, one silver, and two bronz[...]
Olympic medals, in those two events [...]
four different Olympic Games. Sport[...]
Illustrated for Women magazine vote[...]
Joyner-Kersee the Greatest Female
Athlete of the 20th century.

Nat King Cole (1919-1965) Cole, a musician, was born as Nathaniel Adams Coles on March 17, 1919 in Birmingham, Alabama. His 1949 recording of "Mona Lisa" crossed over into the pop charts and sold over three million copies, making him the most successful African-American recording artist at the time.

Mary McLeod Bethune (1875-1955) An educator and co-founder of Bethune-Cookman College, Bethune's work received national attention. She served on two conferences under President Herbert Hoover and was founder of the National Council of Negro women.

George Washington Carver (1861-1943) An African-American educator and agricultural researcher, Carver developed numerous products from the peanut and sweet potato. Among them were plastics, lubricants, facial cream and tapioca.

Daniel Hale Williams (1856-1931)
A pioneer in open heart surgery,
Williams worked on a steamboat and
was a barber before graduating from
Chicago Medical College in 1883.
Williams was instrumental in forming
the National Medical Association and
constructed hospitals and schools
for African-American doctors.

Shirley Chisholm (1924-2005) A congresswoman, public speaker and award winner representing New York, Chisholm was the first African-American woman to serve in Congress. She was elected to the U.S. House of Representatives in 1968. Chisholm made a run for the presidency in 1972 and stated several times she faced more discrimination as a woman than as a black person.

Thurgood Marshall (1908-1993) Marshall was the first African-American to serve on the nation's highest court. In 1967, he was appointed as an associate justice of the United States Supreme Court.